*L*ove is the
source of life

Susan Polis Schutz

Other books in the *"Language of" Series...* by

Blue Mountain Press ®

The Language of Friendship

The Language of Happiness

The Language of Marriage

The Language of Teaching

The Language of Courage and Inner Strength

Thoughts to Share with a Wonderful Mother

Thoughts to Share with a Wonderful Father

Thoughts to Share with a Wonderful Son

Thoughts to Share with a Wonderful Daughter

It's Great to Have a Brother like You

It's Great to Have a Sister like You

The Language of

LOVE

A Collection from Blue Mountain Arts®
Edited by Susan Polis Schutz

Blue Mountain Press ®

Boulder, Colorado

Library of Congress Catalog Card Number: 98-42641
ISBN: 0-88396-478-3

ACKNOWLEDGMENTS appear on page 64.

Manufactured in Thailand
Third Printing: August 1999

♻ This book is printed on recycled paper.

Library of Congress Cataloging-in-Publication Data

The language of love / edited by Susan Polis Schutz.
        p.   cm.
    ISBN 0-88396-478-3 (alk. paper)
      1. Love--Literary collections. I. Schutz, Susan Polis.
PN6071.L7L29 1999
302.3--dc21

                                                98-42641
                                                      CIP

Blue Mountain Press INC.

P.O. Box 4549, Boulder, Colorado 80306

Contents

(Authors listed in order of first appearance)

Love... a small word for such a complex emotion. There is no simple explanation for it, because love is made up of many things. It cannot be measured, because it is a feeling.

All of the money in the world cannot buy love; it has to be earned. It does not happen by wishing; it must come about naturally.

Love is not an instantaneous emotion, but something that grows slowly between two people, maturing with time. Once love has reached maturity, there is no stronger bond between two people.

To love someone means being comfortable and at ease with them, sharing confidences knowing that they will be understood and held in trust. It means respecting each other's dignity and never being demanding, but rather being willing to give, and accepting that which is given, graciously and with love.

To love someone means having a genuine concern for them, being able to sense that something is wrong without being told. It is understanding the other person's problems, moods, and "hang-ups," and accepting all of them even if you don't quite understand. It is excusing their faults, because you know that their good points far outweigh the bad.

Love is always being there for each other with a shoulder to cry on, to give support when confidence levels are low, to give helpful advice when it is asked for, to know when to be silent and just listen, or to give cheerful words of encouragement.

Love is sharing the good and the bad, the hopes and the dreams, the amusing times and the serious times. It is doing things together, yet leaving room for each to grow as an individual.

How do I know these things about love? Because this is the kind of love you have given to me and the kind of love I feel for you.

— Beverly Bruce

If Only You Could Be Me for a Moment...

Sometimes I wish
you could step into my shoes
for just a little while —
  to think what I think;
  to see what I see;
  to feel what I feel;
  to understand the confusion,
  the fear, the admiration, and
  the friendship I feel toward you —
  all at once.

If you were able to live
inside my mind, even for a moment,
you would see that my world is
filled with so many responsibilities,
yet so often my thoughts are of you.
You would see what joy
you've brought to my life.
You would see how much it means to me
to be able to smile, to laugh,
to feel good,
to feel free, like a child —
just because of you.

If you had the chance to take
the smallest glimpse inside of me,
you would see gratitude and respect —
respect not only for what
you are making of yourself,
but also for what
you are helping me to be.
And you would see how much
all of that means to me.

But the thing that would
strike you most —
if ever you had the chance to be me —
would be all the love I feel for you.
And once you had felt it,
you would always remember it,
and you would understand that,
although I am not always able
to express it or to explain
its depth or importance to me,
it is always there... inside of me.

Tracey A. Gibbs

Nothing beats love. Love is the greatest healing power there is, nothing else comes close. Not ancient cures, modern medicines and technologies, or all the interesting books we read or the wise things we say and think. Love has a transformational power.

— Naomi Judd

Love does not consist
in gazing at each other,
but in looking outward
in the same direction.

❀— Antoine de Saint Exupéry

The best way to know life
Is to love many things.

❀❀— Vincent van Gogh

By the accident of fortune a man
    may rule the world for a time,
but by virtue of love he
    may rule the world forever.

He who defends with love
    will be secure;
Heaven will save him, and
    protect him with love.

Kindness in words
        creates confidence.
Kindness in thinking
        creates profoundness.
Kindness in feeling
        creates love.

— Lao Tzu

Take twin mounds of clay,
Mold them as you may.
Shape one after me,
Another after thee.
Then quickly break them both.
Remix, remake them both —
One formed after thee,
The other after me.

Part of my clay is thine;
Part of thy clay is mine.

Kwan Tao-Shing
(13th Century)

Our love was pure
    as the snow on the mountains
White as a moon
    between the clouds.

Cho Wen-Chun

Is the day better than the night?
Or is the night better than the day?
How can I tell?
But this I know is right:
Both are worth nothing
When my love's away.

                                    — Amaru

Although I have a lamp and fire,
Stars, moon, and sun to give me light,
Unless I look into your eyes,
All is dark night.

                                    Bhartrhari

All that we are
is the result of what we think.

How then can a man escape being filled with hatred,
if his mind is constantly repeating.... He misused me,
he hit me, he defeated me, he robbed me — ?

Hatred can never put an end to hatred;
hate is conquered only by love.

— Buddha

Many waters cannot quench love,
nor can the floods drown it.

❀ Song of Solomon 8:7

Entreat me not to leave you,
Or to turn back from following after you;
For wherever you go, I will go;
And wherever you lodge, I will lodge;
Your people shall be my people,
And your God, my God.
Where you die, I will die,
And there will I be buried.
The Lord do so to me, and more also,
If anything but death parts you and me.

❀ Ruth 1:16-17

Love suffers long and is kind;
love does not envy;
love does not parade itself,
is not puffed up;
does not behave rudely,
does not seek its own,
is not provoked, thinks no evil;
does not rejoice in iniquity,
but rejoices in the truth;
bears all things, believes all things,
hopes all things, endures all things.

Love never fails.

1 Corinthians 13:4-8

Let us not love in word or
in tongue, but in deed and in truth.

1 John 3:18

Lighted Lamp

Love is something eternal — the aspect may change, but not the essence. There is the same difference in a person before and after he is in love as there is in an unlighted lamp and one that is burning. The lamp was there and it was a good lamp, but now it is shedding light, too, and that is its real function.

Vincent van Gogh

A soul mate is someone to whom we feel profoundly connected, as though the communicating and communing that takes place between us were not the product of intentional efforts, but rather a divine grace. This kind of relationship is so important to the soul that many have said there is nothing more precious in life.

Thomas Moore

Blow wind, to where my loved one is,
Touch him, and come and touch me soon:
I'll feel his gentle touch through you,
And meet his beauty in the moon.

These things are much for one who loves —
A person can live by them alone —
That he and I breathe the same air,
And that the earth we tread is one.

— Ramayana

The wind that sweeps down Ikaho
One day it blows, they say,
Another it does not blow
Only my love
Knows no time.

— Azumauta

If all the world were mine to plunder
I'd be content with just one town,
And in that town, one house alone,
And in that house, one single room,
And in that room, one cot only,
For there, asleep, is the one I love.

Ancient Sanskrit Poem

It is a good thing to be
rich and to be strong,
but it is a better thing
to be loved.

Euripides

Of all the creations
of the earth and heaven
love is the most precious.

Some say the most beautiful thing
on this dark earth
is a cavalry regiment,
some a battalion of infantry on the march,
and some a fleet of long oars.
But to me the fairest thing is when
one is in love with someone else.

— Sappho
(580 B.C.)

Shall I Compare Thee to a Summer's Day?

Shall I compare thee to a summer's day?
Thou art more lovely and more temperate:
Rough winds do shake the darling buds of May,
And summer's lease hath all too short a date:
Sometime too hot the eye of heaven shines,
And often is his gold complexion dimm'd;
And every fair from fair sometime declines,
By chance or nature's changing course untrimm'd;
But thy eternal summer shall not fade
Nor lose possession of that fair thou owest;
Nor shall Death brag thou wander'st in his shade,
When in eternal lines to time thou growest;
So long as men can breathe or eyes can see,
So long lives this and this gives life to thee.

— William Shakespeare

Love's Not Time's Fool

Let me not to the marriage of true minds
Admit impediments. Love is not love
Which alters when it alteration finds,
Or bends with the remover to remove,
O, no! it is an ever-fixed mark,
That looks on tempests and is never shaken;
It is the star to every wandering bark,
Whose worth's unknown, although his height be taken.
Love's not Time's fool, though rosy lips and cheeks
Within his bending sickle's compass come;
Love alters not with his brief hours and weeks,
But bears it out even to the edge of doom.
If this be error and upon me proved,
I never writ, nor no man ever loved.

—William Shakespeare

There is no difficulty that enough love
will not conquer; No disease that enough love
will not heal; No door that enough love
will not open; No gulf that enough love
will not bridge; No wall that enough love
will not throw down; No sin that enough love
will not redeem...

It makes no difference how deeply seated
may be the trouble,
How hopeless the outlook,
How muddled the tangle,
How great the mistake, —
A sufficient realization of love will dissolve
it all... If only you could love enough,
you would be the happiest and most powerful
being in the world.

Emmet Fox

How do I love thee? Let me count the ways.
I love thee to the depth and breadth and height
My soul can reach, when feeling out of sight
For the ends of Being and ideal Grace.
I love thee to the level of everyday's
Most quiet need, by sun and candle-light.
I love thee freely, as men strive for Right;
I love thee purely, as they turn from Praise.
I love thee with the passion put to use
In my old griefs, and with my childhood's faith.
I love thee with a love I seemed to lose
With my lost saints, — I love thee with the breath,
Smiles, tears, of all my life! — and, if God choose,
I shall but love thee better after death.

Elizabeth Barrett Browning

To My Dear and Loving Husband

If ever two were one, then surely we.
If ever man were loved by wife, then thee;
If ever wife was happy in a man,
Compare with me, ye women, if you can.
I prize thy love more than whole mines of gold
Or all the riches that the East doth hold.
My love is such that rivers cannot quench,
Nor ought but love from thee, give recompense.
Thy love is such I can no way repay,
The heavens reward thee manifold, I pray.
Then while we live, in love let's so persevere
That when we live no more, we may live ever.

Anne Bradstreet

I love you
the more in that I believe
you have liked me for my
own sake and for nothing else.

— John Keats

Every soul is a celestial Venus
to every other soul... Love is our highest
word, and the synonym of God.

— Ralph Waldo Emerson

My Delight and Thy Delight

My delight and thy delight
Walking, like two angels white,
In the gardens of the night:

My desire and thy desire
Twining to a tongue of fire,
Leaping live, and laughing higher;

Through the everlasting strife
In the mystery of life.

Love, from whom the world begun,
Hath the secret of the sun.
Love can tell, and love alone,
Whence the million stars were strewn,
Why each atom knows its own,
How, in spite of woe and death,
Gay is life, and sweet is breath:

This he taught us, this we knew,
Happy in his science true,
Hand in hand as we stood
'Neath the shadows of the wood,
Heart to heart as we lay
In the dawning of the day.

— Robert Bridges

A Birthday

My heart is like a singing bird
Whose nest is in a water'd shoot;
My heart is like an apple tree
Whose boughs are bent with thick-set fruit;
My heart is like a rainbow shell
That paddles in a halcyon sea;
My heart is gladder than all these,
Because my love is come to me.
Raise me a dais of silk and down:
Hang it with fair and purple dyes;
Carve it in doves and pomegranates,
And peacocks with a hundred eyes;
Work it in gold and silver grapes,
In leaves and silver fleurs-de-lis;
Because the birthday of my life
Is come, my love is come to me.

Christina Rossetti

Love Is...

Love is

being happy for the other person when they are happy
being sad for the person when they are sad
being together in good times
and being together in bad times
Love is the source of strength

Love is

being honest with yourself at all times
being honest with the other person at all times
telling, listening, respecting the truth
and never pretending
Love is the source of reality

Love is

an understanding that is so complete that
you feel as if you are a part of the other person
accepting the other person just the way they are
and not trying to change them to be something else
Love is the source of unity

Love is

the freedom to pursue your own desires
while sharing your experiences with the other person
the growth of one individual alongside of
and together with the growth of another individual
Love is the source of success

Love is

    the excitement of planning things together
    the excitement of doing things together
Love is the source of the future

Love is

    the fury of the storm
    the calm in the rainbow
Love is the source of passion

Love is

    giving and taking in a daily situation
    being patient with each other's needs and desires
Love is the source of sharing

Love is

    knowing that the other person
    will always be with you regardless of what happens
    missing the other person when they are away
    but remaining near in heart at all times
Love is the source of security

Love is the

    source of life

Susan Polis Schutz

Love Is...

...light from heaven; A spark of that immortal fire.

— Lord Byron

...the master key that opens the gates of happiness.

— Oliver Wendell Holmes

...a second life; it grows into the soul,
warms every vein, and beats in every pulse.

— Joseph Addison

...to the moral nature exactly what the sun is to the earth.

— Honoré de Balzac

...the beauty of the soul.

— St. Augustine

...the principle of existence and its only end.

— Benjamin Disraeli

...goodness, and honor, and peace and pure living.

— Henry van Dyke

...the dawn of civility and grace.

— Ralph Waldo Emerson

...the enchanted dawn of every heart.

— Alphonse Marie Louis de Lamartine

...the emblem of eternity: it confounds all notion of time: effaces all memory of a beginning, all fear of an end.

— Madame de Stael

...the magician, the enchanter, that changes worthless things to joy.

— Robert Ingersoll

A true relationship
knows of but one great thing:
    to give of one's self
    boundlessly
    in order to find one's self
        richer,
            deeper,
                better.

— Emma Goldman

Let us always
tell each other
our slightest griefs,
our smallest joys...
These confidences,
this exquisite intimacy,
are both the right
and the duty of love.

— Victor Hugo

To renounce your individuality,
   to see with another's eyes,
   to hear with another's ears,
To be two and yet one,
   to so melt and mingle
   that you no longer know
   you are you or another,
To constantly absorb and
   constantly radiate,
To reduce earth, sea and sky
   and all that in them is
   to a single being so wholly
   that nothing whatever is withheld,
To be prepared at any moment
   for sacrifice,
To double your personality
   in bestowing it —
      that is love.

Theophile Gautier

Time Is...

Too Slow for those who Wait,
Too Swift for those who Fear,
Too Long for those who Grieve,
Too Short for those who Rejoice;

But for those who Love,
   Time is Eternity.

—Henry van Dyke

Whoever lives true life, will love true love.

Elizabeth Barrett Browning

That love is all
there is
is all we know of love.

— Emily Dickinson

I love you
not as something private
and personal, which is my own,
but as something universal
and worthy of love
which I have found.

— Henry David Thoreau

Love does not dominate;
it cultivates.

Love has power to give in a
moment what toil can scarcely
reach in an age.

I am so glad that you are here
it helps me to realize how
beautiful my world is.

— Johann Wolfgang von Goethe

It is the true season
of Love
When we know that
we alone can love,
that no one could ever
have loved before us
and that no one
will ever Love
in the same way
after us.

— Johann Wolfgang von Goethe

To love
means to communicate
        to the other
that you are all for him,
that you will never fail him
or let him down
when he needs you,
but that you
will always
be standing by.

Ashley Montagu

I wish I could make you
understand how I love you.
I am always seeking, but
    cannot find a way...

I love in you a something
that only I have discovered —
the you — which is beyond the
    you of the world that is
    admired and known by others;
a "you" which is especially mine;
which cannot ever change,
and which I cannot ever
    cease to love.

                —Guy de Maupassant.

I Love You

I love you,
Not only for what you are
But for what I am
When I am with you.

    I love you
        Not only for what
        You have made of yourself
        But for what
        You are making of me.

I love you
For the part of me
That you bring out;
I love you
For putting your hand
Into my heaped-up heart
And passing over
All the foolish, weak things
That you can't help
Dimly seeing there,
And for drawing out
Into the light
All the beautiful belongings
That no one else had looked
Quite far enough to find.

I love you because you
Are helping me to make
Of the lumber of my life
Not a tavern
But a temple;
Out of works
Of my every day
Not a reproach
But a song.
    I love you
    Because you have done
    More than any creed
    Could have done
    To make me good,
    And more than any fate
    Could have done
    To make me happy.
You have done it
Without a touch,
Without a word,
Without a sign.
    You have done it
    By being yourself.
    Perhaps that is what
    Being a friend means,
    After all.

Roy Croft

Love consists in this
that two solitudes protect
and touch and greet
each other.

There is a miracle that happens every time to those
who really love: the more they give, the more they
possess of that precious nourishing love from which
flowers and children have their strength.

— Rainer Maria Rilke

Nature produces
the greatest results
with the simplest
means. These are
simply the sun,
flowers,
water,
and
love.

— Heinrich Heine

What the heart has once
owned and had, it shall never
lose.

Of all earthly music, that which
reaches the farthest into heaven
is the beating of a loving heart.

— Henry Ward Beecher

Love is the river of life in this world.
Think not that ye know it who stand at the
little tinkling rill, the first small fountain.

Not until you have gone through the rocky
gorges, and not lost the stream; not until you
have gone through the meadow, and the stream
has widened and deepened until fleets could ride
on its bosom; not until beyond the meadow you
have come to the unfathomable ocean, and
poured your treasures into its depths — not
until then can you know what love is.

— Henry Ward Beecher

You and I

My hand is lonely for your clasping, dear;
   My ear is tired waiting for your call.
I want your strength to help, your laugh to cheer;
   Heart, soul and senses need you, one and all.
I droop without your full, frank sympathy;
   We ought to be together — you and I;
We want each other so, to comprehend
   The dream, the hope, things planned, or seen,
      or wrought.
Companion, comforter and guide and friend,
   As much as love asks love, does thought ask thought.
Life is so short, so fast the lone hours fly,
   We ought to be together, you and I.

Henry Alford

The World Is Not
a Pleasant Place to Be

the world is not a pleasant place
to be without
someone to hold and be held by

a river would stop
its flow if only
a stream were there
to receive it

an ocean would never laugh
if clouds weren't there
to kiss her tears

the world is not
a pleasant place to be without
someone

Nikki Giovanni

(17 feb 72)

Outside are the storms and strangers: we —
Oh, close, safe, warm sleep I and she,
— I and she!

Chance cannot change my love,
nor time impair.

What's the earth
With all its art, verse, music, worth
Compared with love, found, gained and kept?

— Robert Browning

When someone cares
it is easier to speak
it is easier to listen
it is easier to play
it is easier to work

When someone cares
it is easier to laugh

— Susan Polis Schutz

love is the every only god

who spoke this earth so glad and big
even a thing all small and sad
man,may his mighty briefness dig

for love beginning means return
seas who could sing so deep and strong

one querying wave will whitely yearn
from each last shore and home come young

so truly perfectly the skies
by merciful love whispered were,
completes its brightness with your eyes

any illimitable star

E. E. Cummings

Some Things I Love

Your enchantment in a lonely wood,
The fight and color of a rainbow trout,
My in-basket empty and a good new book,
Binoculars fixed on a strange new bird,
Sadie's point, and a covey of quail,
The end of a six-mile run in the rain,
Blue slope, soft snow, fast run, no fall,
A dovetail joint without a gap,
Grandchildren coming in our front door,
The same ones leaving in a day or two,
And life, till what rhymes best with breath
takes me from all things I share with you.

— Jimmy Carter

Once I knew the depth where no hope was and darkness lay on the face of all things. Then love came and set my soul free. Once I fretted and beat myself against the wall that shut me in. My life was without a past or future, and death a consummation devoutly to be wished. But a little word from the fingers of another fell into my hands that clutched at emptiness, and my heart leaped up with the rapture of living. I do not know the meaning of the darkness, but I have learned the overcoming of it.

— Helen Keller

Ashes of Life

Love has gone and left me and the days are all alike;
Eat I must, and sleep I will, — and would that night
   were here!
But ah! — to lie awake and hear the slow hours strike!
Would that it were day again! — with twilight near!

Love has gone and left me and I don't know what to do;
This or that or what you will is all the same to me;
But all the things that I begin I leave before I'm through, —
There's little use in anything as far as I can see.

Love has gone and left me, — and the neighbours knock
   and borrow,
And life goes on forever like the gnawing of a mouse, —
And tomorrow and tomorrow and tomorrow and
   tomorrow
There's this little street and this little house.

Edna St. Vincent Millay

The Concert

No, I will go alone.
I will come back when it's over.
Yes, of course I love you.
No, it will not be long.
Why may you not come with me? —
You are too much my lover.
You would put yourself
Between me and song.

If I go alone,
Quiet and suavely clothed,
My body will die in its chair,
And over my head a flame,
A mind that is twice my own,
Will mark with icy mirth
The wise advance and retreat
Of armies without a country,
Storming a nameless gate,
Hurling terrible javelins down
From the shouting walls of a singing town

Where no women wait!
Armies clean of love and hate,
Marching lines of pitiless sound
Climbing hills to the sun and hurling
Golden spears to the ground!
Up the lines a silver runner
Bearing a banner whereon is scored
The milk and steel of a bloodless wound
Healed at length by the sword!

You and I have nothing to do with music.
We may not make of music a filigree frame,
Within which you and I,
Tenderly glad we came,
Sit smiling, hand in hand.

Come now, be content.
I will come back to you, I swear I will;
And you will know me still.
I shall be only a little taller
Than when I went.

Edna St. Vincent Millay

Take Responsibility for Love

To love means being 100 percent responsible for your experience of living, to not be a victim or a martyr, and to be 100 percent accountable for the quality of your life, which includes the amount of love, joy, and growth you create in your relationship each day.

To love is the ability to remain strong, stable, and committed through difficult times, changes, and challenges. It means being gentle, kind, and supportive of your potential, goals, and aspirations.

Love is recognizing that you are powerless to control your love partner. All you can do is take responsibility for yourself. Trying to change him or her through threats, screams, sulks, withdrawal, or hassles will produce negative results. Even if he or she does comply, change occurs at the expense of pride and mutual respect.

Love is assuming at all times that your life mate is good and loving and lovable at his or her essence, and that any negative behavior is learned and a challenge to further understanding.

Harold Bloomfield

The love you seek is seeking you at this moment. Your longing, your deep fantasies about being loved are mere shadows of the melting sweetness that makes spirit want to love you. Be honest about your seeking, and be alert to the moments when love is showing itself to you. You are the only means that love has for conquering its opposition; therefore you are infinitely precious in the eyes of spirit. The messages of love may not be clear to anyone else around you, even those most intimate to you. That doesn't matter; they are meant for you and you alone. Be assured of that.

— Deepak Chopra

I Love You
More Than "Love"

It is impossible to capture in words
the feelings I have for you
They are the strongest feelings that I
have ever had about anything
yet when I try to tell you them
or try to write them to you
the words do not even begin to touch
the depths of my feelings
And though I cannot explain the essence of
these phenomenal feelings
I can tell you what I feel like
when I am with you
When I am with you it is as if
I were a bird
flying freely in the clear blue sky

When I am with you it is as if
   I were a flower
      opening up my petals of life
When I am with you it is as if
   I were the waves of the ocean
      crashing strongly against the shore
When I am with you it is as if
   I were the rainbow after the storm
      proudly showing my colors
When I am with you it is as if
   everything that is beautiful
      surrounds us
This is just a very small part of how wonderful
I feel when I am with you
Maybe the word "love" was invented to explain
the deep, all-encompassing feelings
   that I have for you
but somehow it is not strong enough
But since it is the best word that there is
let me tell you a thousand times that
I love you more than
"love"

 Susan Polis Schutz

ACKNOWLEDGMENTS

We gratefully acknowledge the permission granted by the following authors, publishers, and authors' representatives to reprint poems or excerpts from their publications.

Villard Books, a division of Random House, Inc. for "Nothing beats love..." from LOVE CAN BUILD A BRIDGE by Naomi Judd with Bud Schaetzle. Copyright © 1993 by Naomi Judd. All rights reserved. Reprinted by permission.

HarperCollins Publishers, Inc. for "A soul mate is someone..." from SOUL MATES by Thomas Moore. Copyright © 1994 by Thomas Moore. All rights reserved. Reprinted by permission.

Random House, Inc. for "Love consists in this..." and "There is a miracle..." from LETTERS TO A YOUNG POET by Rainer Maria Rilke, translated and with a foreword by Stephen Mitchell. Copyright © 1984 by Stephen Mitchell. All rights reserved. Reprinted by permission.

William Morrow & Company, Inc. for "The World Is Not a Pleasant Place to Be" from MY HOUSE by Nikki Giovanni. Copyright © 1972 by Nikki Giovanni. All rights reserved. Reprinted by permission.

Liveright Publishing Corporation for "love is the every only god," copyright © 1940, 1968, 1991 by the Trustees for the E. E. Cummings Trust, from COMPLETE POEMS 1904-1962 by E. E. Cummings, edited by George J. Firmage. All rights reserved. Reprinted by permission.

Times Books, a division of Random House, Inc., for "Some Things I Love" from ALWAYS A RECKONING AND OTHER POEMS by Jimmy Carter. Copyright © 1995 by Jimmy Carter. All rights reserved. Reprinted by permission.

Elizabeth Barnett for "Ashes of Life" and "The Concert" by Edna St. Vincent Millay. From COLLECTED POEMS, HarperCollins. Copyright © 1917, 1923, 1945, 1951 by Edna St. Vincent Millay and Norma Millay Ellis. All rights reserved. Reprinted by permission of Elizabeth Barnett, literary executor.

Harold Bloomfield for "Take Responsibility for Love." Copyright © 1996 by Harold Bloomfield. All rights reserved. Reprinted by permission.

Crown Publishers, Inc. for "The love you seek..." from THE PATH TO LOVE by Deepak Chopra. Copyright © 1997 by Deepak Chopra, M.D. All rights reserved. Reprinted by permission.

Scripture quotations in this publication are from the New King James Version. Copyright © 1979, 1980, 1982 by Thomas Nelson, Inc. All rights reserved. Reprinted by permission.

A careful effort has been made to trace the ownership of poems and excerpts used in this anthology in order to obtain permission to reprint copyrighted materials and give proper credit to the copyright owners. If any error or omission has occurred, it is completely inadvertent, and we would like to make corrections in future editions provided that written notification is made to the publisher:

BLUE MOUNTAIN PRESS, INC., P.O. Box 4549, Boulder, Colorado 80306.

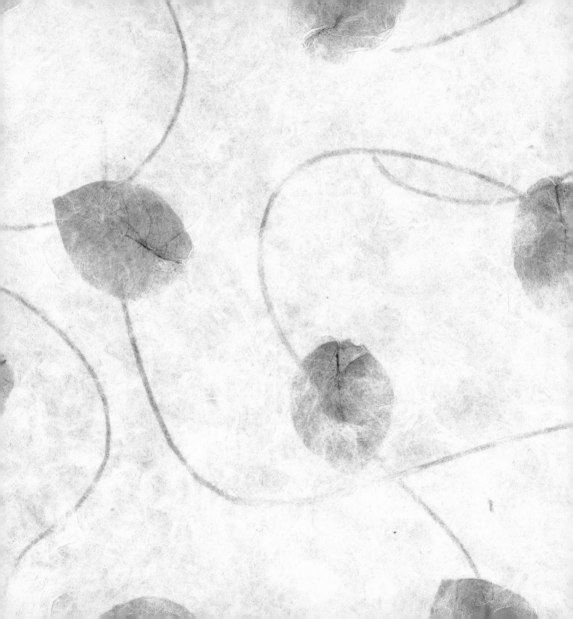